THE MINIATURE BOOK OF

Easter

a Salamander book

Published by Salamander Books Limited
LONDON • NEW YORK

A SALAMANDER BOOK

Published by Salamander Books Ltd
129-137 York Way,
London N7 9LG
United Kingdom

ISBN 0 86101 637 8

Distributed in the United Kingdom by
Hodder and Stoughton Services
PO Box 6, Mill Road
Dunton Green, Sevenoaks
Kent TN13 2YA

All correspondence concerning the content of this volume
should be addressed to Salamander Books Ltd.

CREDITS
Additional Contributors: Rosalind Burdett, Annette Claxton, Jan Hall, Karen
Lansdown, Cheryl Owen, Susy Smith, Sarah Waterkeyn

Editor: *Lisa Dyer*
Photographer: *Steve Tanner*
Illustrator: *Pauline Bayne*
Typesetter: *SX Composing Ltd*
Colour separation: *Scantrans Pte Ltd, Singapore*
Printed in Belgium

Contents

Easter Bonnet Card

A DOLL'S STRAW BONNET
DECORATES THIS PALE
BLUE EASTER CARD

1 Cut a piece of cardboard 15 × 22cm (6 × 8½in), score and fold to 11cm (4¼in). Cut a length of yellow ribbon and cut an inverted 'V' at the ends. Hold in place around a small doll's hat and sew, leaving tails at the back. Repeat with a length of slightly narrower ribbon.

2 Trim stems of small fabric flowers and pin them in place on the ribbon at regular intervals around the hat.

3 Sew flowers in place using doubled thread. Finish by sewing the butterfly on the front. Centre the bonnet on the card and attach by sewing through the brim of the hat, and knotting threads on the inside of the card. A small dab of glue will secure the knots.

Fabergé Egg Card

SEQUINS AND SATIN ADD A
TOUCH OF GLAMOUR TO
A SPECIAL CARD

1 Use a ready-made 3-fold card with an oval, egg-shaped window. Place double-sided tape around the window edges inside the card. Peel off the backing and attach a strip of gold lace. Cut a piece of satin slightly larger than the aperture, and stick it down so the satin side shows through the window.

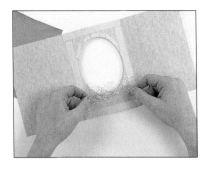

2 Glue a large, jewel-like bead in the centre of the egg. Arrange beads, sequin leaves and petals, then glue in position. Tweezers will make it easier to place the decorations accurately.

3 Finish with a smear of rubber-based glue around the edge of the egg on the outside. Leave for a moment to become tacky, then press down the gold braid firmly. Neatly trim the braid.

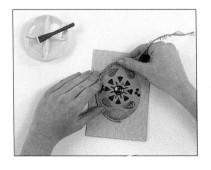

Spring Bouquet

TORN PIECES OF GUMMED
SQUARES MAKE UP THIS
COLOURFUL COLLAGE

12

1 The bouquet on this bright and cheerful greeting card is made up of coloured gummed paper squares torn into simple shapes. Cut a rectangle of white cardboard 38 × 25.5cm (15 × 10in). Score across the centre widthwise using a craft knife. Fold the card in half along the scored line.

2 All the shapes have straight edges. Press a ruler across a gummed square, lift one edge of the paper, and pull it up against the ruler to tear it neatly. Now tear across the paper again, either diagonally or straight across, to form the shapes.

3 Arrange the pieces on the front of the card within a border of narrow strips and squares. Moisten the back of the gummed pieces to stick them in position. Try creating other designs using this method.

Quilted Lilies

THIS SIMPLE QUILTED
PIECE DEPICTS TRADITIONAL
EASTER LILIES

1 To make this piece of quilting, you will need a ready-printed cotton panel, about 10cm (4in) square, and very thin wadding (batting) to back the panel. Pin the panel to a slightly larger square of wadding. Then cut cardboard 45 × 15cm (18 × 6in), and score two folds 15cm (6in) apart.

2 On a larger piece of work, muslin would be used as a backing fabric, but in this instance it has been omitted so there is less bulk inside the card. Working from the centre, tack (baste) the two layers together, making sure the picture covers the wadding.

3 Starting from the centre, with a knot on the back, outline the picture with tiny running stitches. Finish the thread with a double backstitch. Take out the tacking stitches. Measure the finished piece and cut a window from the centre of the 3-fold card. With double-sided tape, stick down the quilted panel and the front flap of card.

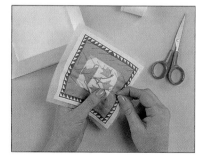

Daffodil Delight

SEW A DAFFODIL PICTURE
TO MAKE INTO A CARD
OR PLACE IN A FRAME

1 Cut a piece of cardboard 22cm (8½in) square, then score and fold at 11cm (4¼in). Cut out a window 9 × 16.5cm (3½ × 6½in). Trace daffodils from a catalogue or book, and transfer on to cartridge paper. Paint with transfer paints. When dry, place over a square of polyester fabric and press with a hot dry iron for two minutes. Carefully lift off the paper.

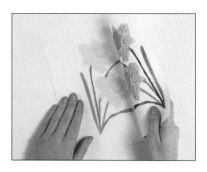

2 Place the print in an embroidery frame the opposite way from hand embroidery, and pull until taut. To machine embroider, use the same thread on the top and the bobbin. Take off the presser foot and drop the 'feed dog' so you will be able to move the work freely. Place the embroidery ring under the needle and drop the pressure lever.

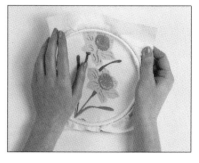

3 Moving the machine wheel by hand, draw up the bobbin thread to the top and hold it to start. Move ring, keeping your fingers on the edge of the frame and slowly paint with your needle. Sew the outline first, then colour in. Experiment with different stitches. Press on the reverse side, mount with double-sided tape and back with white paper.

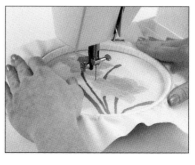

Bunny Egg Warmer

MAKE A BREAKFAST-TIME
BUNNY TO BRING CHEER
TO EASTER MORNING

1 This cute little bunny can be popped over a soft-boiled egg to keep it warm. First cut out two bunny shapes in white felt. Cut the ears from pink felt, the waistcoat from yellow, and the nose and eyes from black. Glue them in place. Embroider the mouth and whiskers in black thread. Glue on sequins for the buttons and the eyes.

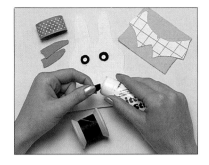

2 Take a piece of ribbon 5cm (2in) long and glue the ends together to form a loop. Tie a piece of thread tightly around the middle of the ribbon to form a bow, and sew it to the rabbit between the mouth and the top of the waistcoat.

3 With the wrong sides facing, sew the front and back felt pieces together along the edge, using a blanket stitch.

Chirpy Chicks

THESE CHEERFUL CHICKS
WILL GUIDE GUESTS TO
THEIR SEATS

1 Following the chick shape in the main picture, cut out a chick in lemon-coloured cardboard, creating a tab at the bottom of the chick's body. Cut out a beak and feet in orange cardboard. Glue the beak to the chick and draw the eyes with a black felt-tipped pen.

2 Write the name of your guest with a pencil diagonally on the chick using a letter stencil. Fill in the letters with a felt-tipped pen.

3 Score a sliver of the cardboard along the bottom of the chick's body and bend the tab backward at a right angle. Glue the tab to the chick's feet.

Egg Place Marker

PAINT A HAND-BLOWN EGG
TO CREATE A USEFUL
TABLE DECORATION

1 To make this unusual place marker, pierce the top of an egg with a pin and the bottom with a darning needle, plunging the needle well in to break the yolk. Hold the egg over a cup and blow through the smaller hole, forcing the contents out through the bottom. Carefully rinse the shell. Pencil on the name and design.

2 Using a white water-based paint, fill in all the areas that will be painted in light colours. This will help to ensure that the colours are true.

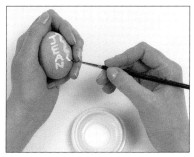

3 Use your chosen colours to paint over the white areas. There is no need to worry if the outline is untidy, since the darker background will cover all the edges. Finally, paint the background in a dark colour.

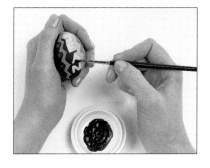

Gift Baskets

TINY TABLE BASKETS
FILLED WITH TREATS ARE
AN EASTER DELIGHT

24

1 You will need a sheet of paper 20cm (8in) square. Fold the square in half diagonally, then diagonally again. Place the triangle with the single fold running vertically. Bring the upper of the two free points up to meet the single point, opening the flap out as you do so to form a square. Crease the folds and repeat on the other side.

2 Position the newly formed square with the free edges pointing away from you. Fold the top free corner down to meet the opposite corner, then fold it back on itself to the horizontal centre line. Fold in half once more. Repeat on the other side, as shown. Turn the top left flap over to the right side, then fold it back on itself to meet the vertical centre line.

3 Fold the left hand corner in towards the vertical line also. Turn the basket over and repeat on the other side. Open out the shape slightly and fold the top two flaps down inside the basket. Flatten the base of the basket. Cut a thin strip of paper for a handle and slip the ends into the slots on each side of the basket rim. Staple in place and decorate with ribbons or lace.

Ribbon Tablecloth

PASTEL-COLOURED RIBBONS
ARE USED TO ADORN A
SIMPLE PURPLE TABLECLOTH

1 To make this project, start with either a ready-made tablecloth or one you have sewn yourself. Buy enough ribbon in each colour to run along four sides of the cloth, plus 24cm (8in) if using a ready-made cloth. Position the ribbons as shown, with fusible webbing underneath (omitting the area where the ribbons cross) and pin them in place.

2 Continue to pin the ribbons in place along all the edges, making sure that you keep them straight. Thread the ribbons underneath one another to create a lattice effect, as shown. If you are using a ready-made cloth, allow the ribbons to overlap the edge by 2.5cm (1in); this will be folded under later.

3 Replace the corner pins with tacking (basting) stitches, if you are working on an unhemmed cloth; this provides extra stability. Press the ribbons in place with a warm iron, removing pins as you go and stopping just short of the tacking. Finally, hem the edges. On a ready-made cloth, sew the ribbon ends to the wrong side by hand.

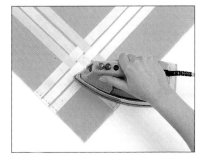

Easter Egg Gift

THIS EGG-SHAPED GIFT
BOX IS FILLED WITH
PRETTY DRIED FLOWERS

1 The flowers in this Easter gift have been specially chosen to reflect the colours of the egg-shaped box, creating a co-ordinated effect. Cut a section from a sphere of florists' foam and put it in the base. Secure with tape. Place the lid about a third of the way across the foam and again tape in place.

2 Build up the outline using brown grass and green amaranthus (love-lies-bleeding). Use some of the amaranthus leaves to add a contrast of texture. Intersperse the display with a few small bunches of tiny red helichrysum, placing them deep into the arrangement.

3 To finish, dot a number of South African daisies (a form of helichrysum) throughout the arrangement. Provided the stems are strong, these can be added singly without wiring.

Spring Chick

A BRIGHT YELLOW POM-POM
CHICK ADDS CHARM TO
AN EASTER GIFT

1 This cheery chick will brighten up any Easter gift. Cut two cardboard circles the same size, then cut a small circle from the centre of each. Put both rings together and wind yellow yarn around them, passing the yarn through the centre. Continue until the rings are well covered and the inner circle is almost full of yarn.

2 Snip through all the yarn along the outer edge of the rings. Pass a length of yarn between the two rings, wind it tightly around all the strands and tie it firmly, leaving long ends. Cut off the cardboard circles. Make a bigger ball for the body from two larger rings and, before cutting, pass a pipe cleaner through the rings to form 'legs'.

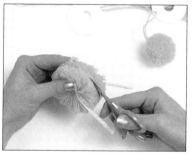

3 Tie the two balls together firmly. Bend the 'legs' up at the ends and wind a section of pipe cleaner around each foot, leaving a 'V' shape on either side so each foot has three 'claws'; paint the feet and legs red. Make eyes and a beak out of felt and glue into position.

Flower Baskets

BASKETS FILLED WITH
FLOWERING PLANTS MAKE
ATTRACTIVE CENTREPIECES

1 These pretty baskets make a delightful centrepiece. First line the basket with a piece of plastic, using black for a dark basket or white for a light-coloured basket. Add a layer of damp sphagnum moss. This will prevent the roots of the plants from drying out.

2 You can leave the basket plain or, as shown here, add a paper doily for a pretty trim. Cut two doilies in half and fold the edge of each half around the rim of the basket before inserting the flower pots.

3 Arrange the plants on top of the layer of moss, adjusting them if necessary so that they will relate well to each other. Then tie ribbons around the handle of each basket to provide the finishing touch.

Host of Daffodils

A BIG BUNCH OF THESE
YELLOW DAFFODILS MAKES A
LONG-LASTING DISPLAY

1 For the base of each daffodil head, cut a section from an egg box (carton) and trim it down to an even edge. Use a yellow one if you can, or else paint it yellow. Next take a flexible paper or plastic straw and roll it in a strip of green tissue, gluing both long edges. Trim the ends and bend the straw without tearing the paper.

2 Insert the stem through the daffodil base. Then cut out some yellow tissue petals and glue first one row, then a second, around the inside of the yellow egg box base.

3 Finally scrunch up a small piece of orange tissue paper and glue it to the centre of the flower. Make a bunch of the daffodil flowers for an extravagant display.

Silver Tree

FOR A STUNNING EFFECT
DECORATE A SILVER BRANCH
WITH SILK FLOWERS

1 Spring is in the air with a shiny silver pot plant, blossoming with pink flowers. For this project, you need a small plastic pot and a small, graceful tree branch. Spray them both with silver paint.

2 Push the silver branch into the middle of a block of modelling clay and fix the clay into the pot. If necessary, weight the base of the clay with a stone for stability. For the 'earth' scrunch up a piece of silver foil and arrange it around the base of the branch.

3 For the blossoms you need little pink silk flowers, scrunched up pink tissue paper, green tissue leaves, and pink and green gift wrap ribbon. Glue these along the branch as shown, spacing them to look reasonably realistic.

Apricots & Cream

APRICOTS, FREESIAS AND
IVY MAKE AN EYE-CATCHING
DISPLAY ON A GLASS STAND

1 A mound of luscious apricots, flowers and leaves makes a pretty centrepiece for a spring buffet or dinner party. Place a white doily on a glass or china cake stand. Carefully push ivy leaves underneath the edge of the doily. The leaves should be washed and can be wiped with cooking oil for extra shine.

2 Holding the doily in place with one hand, arrange the apricots in a pile. If the apricots are to be eaten, do not allow them to touch the ivy leaves, which are poisonous. Then arrange a few sprays of cream-coloured freesias around the pile of apricots.

3 Finally, slot flowers into the gaps between the apricots – any small cream or white flowers will do; those used here are narcissi. Check with your florist that the flowers you choose are not poisonous.

Flowers in a Hat

REVIVE A STRAW HAT
BY USING IT AS A BASE
FOR A FLOWER ARRANGEMENT

1 To start, tape some soaked florists' foam to a saucer and place it in an old straw bonnet. Create a soft and spidery outline with stems of sprengeri fern. Next, take three or four stems of white stock and insert them into the heart of the display, bringing just one stem forward over the brim of the hat.

2 Use white chrysanthemums to fill in the outline and give substance to the design. Generally, chrysanthemums are good survivors when cut, but they will last even longer if the stems are placed into boiling water before being inserted in deep water for a long drink.

3 In among the white chrysanthemums recess some lilac hyacinth heads to create depth and a contrasting texture. Finally, complete the display with deep purple anemones. These are the main flowers, so use plenty, spreading them evenly throughout the whole arrangement.

Spring Sunshine

SUNNY YELLOW PROVIDES A
PERFECT BACKDROP FOR
BRIGHT FLOWERS

1 Prop open the lid of a yellow case with a small stick, and insert a brick of soaked florists' foam wrapped in cling film (plastic wrap). Begin by grouping some closely cut, white iris to the right of the case, standing them upright at the back. Next to them, insert a bunched piece of white net.

2 In front of the iris, group eight to ten yellow Persian buttercups and a touch of foliage. Six or seven white double tulips fill virtually the rest of the case. Retain their leaves, as these add an attractive contrast of colour to the display.

3 On the far left of the case, and in among the tulips, slot three or four purple hyacinths. For the finishing touch, add a little piece of lilac net, bunched on some wire, in the top right hand corner to balance the colour scheme.

Chick Mobile

LITTLE FLUFFY POM-POM
CHICKS MAKE A CHARMING
MOBILE FOR A ROOM

1 For each chick, you need two pom-poms (see page 31 for instructions). For the larger pom-pom use cardboard circles 6cm (2½in) in diameter with 2.5cm (1in) holes. The small circles are 5cm (2in) across with the same size hole. When the larger one is ready to be cut away, push a pipe cleaner through the hole to form the legs and feet.

2 Now cut and tie the pom-poms, joining the head and body together by tying the spare yarn tightly. Make one or two stitches through the head and body to hold them in place.

3 Trim each chick with a felt beak and wings, and a feather for the tail, sticking them on with a dab of glue. Tie a piece of shirring elastic around the neck, and use it to attach a piece of rickrack or ribbon to the chick. Then hang it to two crossed sticks, tied together. Glue the rickrack in place to prevent the chicks from slipping.

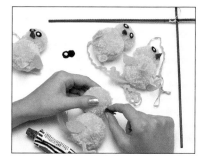